The SELF-CONFIDENCE DEVOTIONAL FOR YOUTH

AGES 7-12

A 30-DAY JOURNEY OF BUILDING WORTH, CONFIDENCE AND CHARACTER

BY LINDSAY M. WARREN, MD

Trafford rev. 01/18/2022

 **www.trafford.com**
North America & international
toll-free: 844-688-6899 (USA & Canada)
fax: 812 355 4082

THE SELF-CONFIDENCE DEVOTIONAL FOR YOUTH
- A 30-Day Journey of Building Worth, Confidence and Character -

Table of Contents

Dedication

To my beautiful and brilliant daughters:

Grace, Charis, and Hannah, thank you for inspiring me to create, write and evolve.

I love you today, tomorrow, and forever and there is nothing you can do to change it!

Acknowledgments

To my husband, Gareth: I love you. Thank you for being an amazing husband, father, and leader.

Special thanks to my editors: Tia Ragland Medley M.D., Edna Connally D.Min., and Kelley Carroll M.D. Your unique input has been priceless. I am grateful for your careful review and prayerful insight.

Many thanks to my illustrator, Chris House: I am grateful for your artistic, creative expression and design. It was great to work with you.

For You are my hope; O Lord God, You are my trust from my youth and the source of my confidence.

— *Psalm 71:5 (AMPC)*

Introduction Part 1: Letter to The Parents

(Kids Have Permission To Read This Too)

"While the earth remains, seed time and harvest, cold and heat, summer and winter, day and night, shall not cease." *Genesis 8:22 NKJV*

Dear Parents,

If you are like me, you want to maximize this brief yet impactful season with your children. During this critical time, I think it's important for us to remember that the Word of God is just as precious and powerful in the lives of our kids, as it is in the lives of their parents (you and I). Everything I have written in this book, I consider to be a "seed" that will be planted in the most important soil we have been gifted, our children. I was inspired to write this kids devotional for several reasons. I recognize the importance of building worth, confidence, and character at a young age and that these *seeds* will grow and develop to produce a great foundation, as our young people mature. The magnitude of having our children confess God's Word, while praying directly to God for themselves cannot be understated. I understand that tools like this book are necessary to help our kids overcome various cultural, ethnic, gender or socio-economic biases or discrimination that they may be exposed to in various environments.

Endeavoring to help my own daughters cultivate their relationship with the Lord and help them supersede all these barriers, inspired the words of this book. It is my intention that this book will instill inner strength to conquer competition, comparison, and other challenges. My prayer is that this book will empower them to crush the mental battles that plague young people (and even little people) regarding their appearance, popularity, social media, identity, and popular culture. My husband and I are in the process of raising three amazing girls to be amazing kingdom women. I believe this devotional will empower our next generation, to walk in godly character and confidence. As a parent, I want to thank you for allowing me the privilege of sharing these truths with your sons and daughters. I believe the incorruptible seed of the Word of God will, over the course of their lives, produce good fruit of God's love, God's encouragement, and God's purpose for their lives.

We are called to sow seeds of integrity, virtue, wisdom and worth into our children. As they read the passages that I've prepared for each day and pray the outlined prayers with a pure heart, I believe an understanding of their great value and individual uniqueness will become very real to them. This information will be the foundation for the conversations around their personal relationships and choices later in their life's journey. Our children are indeed, worth the wait, for God's plan, His purpose, His calling, His timing, and the future covenant relationship that awaits them, should they choose to embrace it.

This book is entitled the "self-confidence" book because Jesus was very clear that you should love your neighbor as you love your**SELF** (*Matthew 22:39 NKJV*). The words used to intentionally build self-confidence, self-worth, self-esteem, and self-love are paramount to the heart of this book. Unfortunately, I believe that we have seen a generation of young people that do not *like* themselves and consequently, do not *love* themselves. This has made it equally difficult for many of them to make healthy decisions. One of my goals with this book, is to counteract those poor self-images and even the negative self-talk that can begin at such a young age.

In summary, please dive into this book with your young person. Each day's reading will include a section called "Parental/Adult Engagement". This section will offer suggested questions that will help facilitate the conversation you should have with your young person after the reading. Feel free to use questions of your own.

I simply want to provide a basic framework that will encourage the dialogue. At the end of this 30-day journey, I have written a SELF-CONFIDENCE DECLARATION. Please allow your child to sign it and even cut it out, as a reminder of the significance of this self-confidence journey. Making it a daily declaration would be a great way to continue the process of affirming them for years to come.

I am praying that this book will be a life-changing pivotal point for great things to come. I am praying that this book will establish worth, confidence and character that is rooted in God's love for your young person.

Sincerely in Him,

Lindsay M. Warren, MD

Anesthesiologist, Author, Speaker,
Founder of Worth The Wait Revolution, Inc

www.iamworththewait.com

Introduction Part 2: Letter To The Kids

Hey my friend!

I am super excited about you beginning this journey with me! It is *not* by chance that you are reading my book at this moment in your life. God wants to use this book to bring you closer to Him. I have written this book just for YOU. God loves YOU and wants you to get to know Him, more and more. This 30-day journey will focus on building your worth, confidence, and character with the Word of God. I will also provide some additional words to encourage you and challenge your thinking. As you are reading, please be open to the wisdom and advice that I will share. The things I have written in this book are being shared to help you grow and develop into the amazing person that God has designed you to be. At times, I may share stories from my younger years to help you understand my journey and why I am so passionate about helping you along your journey. I am also a Mom of three girls, and just like some of the adults in your life, I want my kids to REALLY get to know God and how much He loves them, too. So, if someone has given you this book to read, it's because they deeply care for you, and they truly want the best for you. Ok!!

Now, let's discuss how to read this book. Here is a helpful guide to your daily reading:

1) Start at the beginning with **Day 1**, which is letter **"A"**.

2) Read through the entire Day's message, because it will focus on one central theme. For example, **Day 1** which is letter **A**, focuses on the word **"AWESOME"**.

3) **The Declaration** is the part that you say out loud to yourself. I want you to speak these words as a personal affirmation. These words will build you up and encourage you. Speak these words and as you say them, listen to them and let them sink down into your heart. Over time, these words will change your life.

4) Read the **Scriptures of Worth, Confidence and Character** to help give you a deeper connection with God's word and His special thoughts about you.

5) Read the **Words of Worth, Confidence and Character** which will help you understanding more about this journey and how important you are to God, your family, and this generation.

6) **Prayer** is the next section and it will lead you in a personal prayer to God about the topic you just read. Please pray the prayers that have been written for you, as they will help connect you with God and begin the process of building your worth, confidence, and character in Him.

7) **Parental/Adult Engagement** section gives an adult the opportunity to ask you a few questions about what you have read, to make sure you are grasping the material and understanding how to properly apply it to your life.

8) Repeat this process each day until you have completed all 30 days of the journey. Even after you have completed the book, feel free to read, again and start from the beginning, to build even more self-confidence that is rooted in the Word of God.

At the very end of the book, you will see the **SELF-CONFIDENCE DECLARATION**. It is a summary of all the daily affirmations listed in the book. Feel free to cut out this page of the book (with your parent's permission) and post this declaration in a location that you visit frequently. You can sign it, date it and speak these words over your life every single day. It will remind you of this journey and maintain your self-confidence during every season of your life.

I'm so excited and I'm looking forward to enjoying this journey with you. Feel free to include your parents, pastors, or mentors on this reading journey as well.

Big hugs and much love!

Dr. Lindsay

Day 1
A
AWESOME

Declaration: "I AM AWESOME!"

Scriptures of Worth, Confidence and Character:
"And, he said, Behold, I am making a covenant. Before all
your people I will do marvels, such as have not been done
in all the earth, nor in any nation; and all the people among
whom you are shall see the work of the Lord. For it is an
awesome thing that I will do with you." *Exodus 34:10 NKJV*

Words of Worth, Confidence and Character:
You are awesome!

You are amazing. God loves you and He has a great
plan and purpose for your life. Begin to think about
all the possibilities and the potential that you uniquely
possess. You are a miracle that God has allowed to be
born for this time and for this generation. This world
will not be the same without your unique and special
contributions. You may feel like just a young person,
but God has big things in store for your life. When I was
a little girl, I always wanted to become a doctor, but I
didn't always know how God was going to bring that
dream to pass. But as I went through school, step by
step, the Lord helped me and opened special doors for
me to become an anesthesiologist. An anesthesiologist
is the doctor that puts patients to sleep for surgery and
keeps them safe during the entire procedure. I play
an important role in the lives of my patients and I am
thankful that God has given me the skills and the ability
to do it.

Also, I had no idea that one day I would become an author and that people would actually want to read my books. Yet, here I am as a published author and helping young people like you, with my writing. Cool, right? I always thought that in life, you had to pick just one goal or one job or one profession and just do one thing for the rest of your life. Yet God is so big and His plan for you is so interesting that what He has planned can really surprise you. I'm so grateful to have this moment to encourage you through this book. You never know what "greatness" God has in store for you.

Dream big dreams, think great thoughts, and expect good things. Right now, is the beginning of your journey to understanding how important it is for you to build your character and your confidence around the Word of God. Begin to thank God for the gift of life, your talents, your strengths, and all the special things that make you, awesome. As the scripture says, "…it is an awesome thing that I will do with you." Your family, your community and your world are excited to see the awesome things that are yet to come!

Prayer: Lord, I love You and I'm so grateful for the awesome plan that You have for my life. Even as a young person, I begin my journey of trusting You with my future. Let Your will be done, today and every day, in the name of Jesus. Amen.

Parental/Adult Engagement:
What 3-5 awesome things can you see yourself doing in the future? What does it mean to dream big dreams and expect good things throughout your journey?

Personal Notes/Personal Thoughts:

_____
_____
_____
_____
_____
_____
_____
_____
_____
_____
_____
_____
_____
_____
_____
_____
_____
_____
_____
_____
_____
_____
_____
_____
_____
_____
_____
_____
_____
_____
_____

Day 2
B
BRILLIANT

Declaration: "I AM BRILLIANT!"

Scriptures of Worth, Confidence and Character:
"You are the light of the world. A city that is set on a hill cannot be hidden. Nor do they light a lamp and put it under a basket, but on a lamp stand, and it gives light to all who are in the house. Let your light so shine before men, that they may see your good works and glorify your Father in heaven." *Matthew 5:14-16 NKJV*

Words of Worth, Confidence and Character:
You are brilliant!

The word brilliant has two meanings. It can describe a person of high intelligence or an object that reflects light. For this discussion, you are the object that reflects the Light of the World, Jesus Christ. You are a bright light shining in your family, your community, and this generation. God wants you to shine bravely and boldly so that others will see His goodness in your life, and they will in turn desire a relationship with Him. As a younger kid, I didn't really have a strong relationship with the Lord, so I couldn't really shine brightly for Him. I didn't read or understand much of the bible. At times, I made poor choices and disobeyed my parents. It wasn't until I was a little bit older that my personal relationship with the Lord began.

My parents and my siblings noticed a great change that was taking place in my life. They could see the change in my attitude, my words, and my behavior. I started reading my bible on my own, praying, and becoming a bright light for others in my family. My younger sister and brother were two of the first people that I began to really share my faith with.

No matter how old or young you are, God has called you and I "... the light of the world." Together, as we all shine brilliantly, we can change the darkness around us.

Prayer: Lord, I love You. Help me to be a brilliant light that shines before people and gives You glory and honor. I'm grateful to be a bright light for You, in the name of Jesus. Amen.

Parental/Adult Engagement:
What does this message about being *'brilliant'* mean to you? How can you apply it to your life now?

Personal Notes/Personal Thoughts:

_____

_____

_____

_____

_____

_____

_____

_____

_____

_____

_____

_____

_____

_____

_____

_____

_____

_____

_____

Day 3
C
CREATIVE

Declaration: "I AM CREATIVE!"

Scriptures of Worth, Confidence and Character:
"For by Him all things were created that are in heaven and that are on the earth, visible and invisible, whether thrones or dominions or principalities or powers. All things were created through Him and by Him." *Colossians 1:16 NKJV*

Words of Worth, Confidence and Character:
You are creative!

Just think, the God of the universe that used His amazing creative power to form the heaven, earth, moon, stars, and all creatures, also used His creativity to make YOU! Even as He is creative and the source of all creativity, He has put that same creativity on the inside of you, to be and to do the amazing things He has purposed for you. Your destiny is connected to your creativity. There are special ways that you write, draw, speak, dance, think, share, build, lead and inspire others and you will continue to discover more about your creative strengths as you grow and develop. When I was a kid, I performed in my school play, participated in a few gymnastic events, sang in the children's church choir, wrote a book with my teacher, and played the clarinet. I even had a few ballet and swim classes. I had many interests and wanted to explore all these different creative ways of expression. I am thankful for my parents' support during those discovery years. As you continue to develop your relationship with God, you will see how your unique creativity is a gift from Him.

Your life is an exciting journey of learning more about how He has created you. Trying new things will help you figure out the activities that you enjoy versus the things that do not interest you. Trying new things will also help you to understand your likes versus your dislikes. My daughter Grace loves to sing and so she is taking singing lessons to explore that creative side of her personality. My daughter Charis really likes gymnastics, science, and cooking, so she is always exploring new recipes and experiments. My daughter Hannah Love is the youngest, but she is shaping up to be a great leader and thinker. There are no limits to what God has called and created you to do and its never too early or too late to start considering the many possibilities for greatness that are ahead of you.

Prayer: Lord, I love You and I thank You for creating me and placing Your creativity on the inside of me. I am created in Your image and in Your likeness. Help me to creatively fulfill my purpose all the days of my life, in Jesus' name. Amen.

Parental/Adult Engagement:
What are some of your creative strengths and abilities? Are there any new things that you would like to creatively explore that may help you discover your unique purpose?

Personal Notes/Personal Thoughts:

_____

_____

_____

_____

_____

_____

_____

Day 4
D
DELIGHTFUL

Declaration: "I AM DELIGHTFUL!"

Scriptures of Worth, Confidence and Character:
"As for the saints who are on the earth, they are the excellent ones in whom is all my delight." *Psalms 16:3 NKJV*

Words of Worth, Confidence and Character:
You are delightful!

I love it when one of my girls just starts a random conversation with me about the things going on in their world. I enjoy chatting like we are buddies because we are. I think it's such a cool moment when we get to talk about what their minds want to discuss. The best part is that they actually want to connect, with me, their Mom. I delight in my girls, the same way that God delights in YOU. Did you know that God enjoys your friendship and your conversation? Did you know that He is happy to hear your voice when you pray, when you sing or when you simply chat with Him in your own unique way? Always remember that God loves you and enjoys your company. It makes Him smile when you come close to learn more about Him and His plans for you.

From the very beginning of time, He has always wanted to have a close relationship with you and to walk with you during your life's journey. This is what makes you so delightful! Your family and loved ones are also blessed to be able to walk alongside you and share in your life story. You are full of great things that will be discovered as your life begins to unfold into God's perfect plan.

So, don't be afraid to just talk to God and have random conversations with Him, like my kids do with me. God isn't angry or upset with you. He loves you and looks forward to talking about silly things as well as serious things. He is a loving and concerned Heavenly Father that truly enjoys spending time with us, His children.

Prayer: Lord, I love You and I am grateful that You delight in me and long to be my friend. It makes me happy to know that You want to be close to me. Help me to learn more about You and how to delight in You as well, in Jesus' name. Amen.

Parental/Adult Engagement:
Do you realize how much God likes you and wants to be your friend?

Personal Notes/Personal Thoughts:

_____

_____

_____

_____

_____

_____

_____

_____

_____

_____

_____

_____

_____

_____

_____

_____

_____

Day 5
E
EXCELLENT

Declaration: "I AM EXCELLENT!"

Scriptures of Worth, Confidence and Character:
"Then this Daniel distinguished himself above the governors and satraps because an excellent spirit was in him; and the king gave thought to setting him over the whole realm." *Daniel 6:3 NKJV*

Words of Worth, Confidence and Character:
You are excellent!

Daniel was a young man that out-shined others around him because God gave him special favor, skills, and wisdom. His "excellence" was a direct result of his close relationship with God. Daniel maintained his relationship and intimacy with God above everything in his life. I will be very honest with you. I have never felt like I was "excellent" in life or "excellent" at anything. I usually felt average or above average in school, sports, singing, dancing, and performing. I was good at a lot of things, but never truly excellent. Teachers, principals, coaches, and leaders usually liked me, but I never really cared enough to give a consistent 100% effort towards the things in my life, like my clarinet lessons (which I started in the 5th grade), piano lessons, gymnastics, basketball, volleyball or even my track events.

At times I wonder if my life would be different today if I had been motivated to be excellent like Daniel. Every day, Daniel remained close with the Lord through prayer and allowed His relationship with God to be demonstrated through his everyday life. His hard work, focus, consistency, service, great attitude, and overall performance was extraordinary. Working hard and showing dedication to the important things in your life, demonstrate that an excellent spirit is in you, as well. Daniel's life was extremely blessed with special opportunities, promotion, and success, because of his excellence. Being great at something doesn't just happen overnight. Being great takes commitment, sacrifice and personal effort. This type of excellence gets the attention of others, but most importantly it also represents God in a special way that makes Him proud.

Prayer: Lord, I love You! Please help me to be excellent for You. Like Daniel, help me to be excellent in school, at home, in my behavior, in my activities and every area of my life. As I am excellent, for Your glory, I pray that others will be blessed and want to know more about You, in Jesus' name. Amen.

Parental/Adult Engagement:
What does this message on being 'excellent' mean to you? Can you apply this to any areas of your life?

Personal Notes/Personal Thoughts:

_____

_____

_____

_____

_____

_____

_____

_____

_____

_____

Day 6
F
FEARLESS

Declaration: "I AM FEARLESS!"

Scriptures of Worth, Confidence and Character:
"Have I not commanded you? Be strong and of good courage; do not be afraid, nor be dismayed, for the Lord your God is with you wherever you go." *Joshua 1:9 NKJV*

"For God has not given us a spirit of fear, but of power and of love and of a sound mind." *2 Timothy 1:7 NKJV*

Words of Worth, Confidence and Character:
You are fearless!

As a kid, I remember being afraid of failure. I feared failure in school subjects. I also feared that I would fail at performing well in the sports I played. I feared that my abilities wouldn't be 'perfect'. I had a fear of letting people down. I guess in some ways you could have described me as a 'people-pleaser'. This is someone who needs the approval, applause, and acceptance of others to feel good about themselves. I felt that way when I was younger and have even felt that way sometimes as an adult. I've had to learn that God is always with me and that His grace is more than enough for my failures and imperfections.

Your worth is not tied to the approval, applause, and acceptance of others. Your worth is rooted and grounded in God's love for you. In the passage you just read, a young man named Joshua was preparing to do something new, something challenging and something he felt unqualified to do. But God spoke these very words to him, just as He speaks them to you, right now. You must know that God instructs you to be strong, brave, and courageous, even when you "feel" fearful. Why? You must remember that you are never alone, and that God promises to be with you. You can face anything knowing that He is by your side and that He cares for you, always. No matter what happens, He has your back and will keep you. Remember, God has given you a spirit of power, love, and a sound mind. That means He is with you; He is for you, and He is on your side. He will face all challenges with you. You can trust Him with school stuff, your parents, your family issues, or anything that comes your way. God's grace will be more than enough to conquer your fear of failure or any other fear. So, be strong and be courageous, my friend, for the Lord is with you everywhere you go and in all that you do.

Prayer: Lord, I love You and I thank You for Your promise of being with me everywhere I go. I have victory over my fears, and I trust You to help me and give me courage in the face of fear, in Jesus' name. Amen.

Parental/Adult Engagement:
What are some of the fears that you can give to the Lord, in exchange for His courage? What does this message on being *'fearless'* mean to you and how can you apply it to your life?

Personal Notes/Personal Thoughts:

_____

_____

_____

_____

_____

_____

Day 7
G
GIFTED

Declaration: "I AM GIFTED!"

Scriptures of Worth, Confidence and Character:
"Every good and perfect gift is from above, coming down from the Father of heavenly lights..." *James 1:17 NIV*

"For the gifts and callings of God are irrevocable." *Romans 11:29 NKJV*

"A man's gift makes room for him and brings him before great men." *Proverbs 18:16 NKJV*

Words of Worth, Confidence and Character:
You are gifted!

All your amazing gifts come from God. Can you sing? Can you play football? Can you dance? Can you recite poetry? Can you draw? Can you create art? Can you solve problems? Can you heal others? Can you speak well? Can you act? Can you serve others well? Can you build and create? Can you share the good news of Jesus with others? Can you play tennis? Can you solve complex math equations? Can you engineer new things? Can you design clothes? Can you care for others? Can you serve the homeless? Can you play the piano? Can you play the guitar? Can you lead others? Can you make people laugh? The list of amazing gifts from God goes on and on.

As a kid, I was a friendly person and people liked me. I had friends from school, church, sports, and girl scouts. God gave me many friends from different backgrounds.

As I got older, I realized that God made me a friendly, easy-going, likable person for His purpose. People have always been naturally drawn to me, and it creates an opportunity for them to see Jesus through my life. Even that is a gift from God.

Take a moment to think about 2-3 things that you do well. The things that you do well are gifts and strengths. Begin to recognize at a young age that all these gifts, talents and abilities come from God and that He is the source of your strength. Along with the help of your loved ones, begin to develop your gifts, learn more about your God-given strengths and pray about how God would like to use them now and in the future. Great things are in your future my friend.

Prayer: Lord, I love You and I'm excited about the gifts you have placed on the inside of me. Please begin to reveal these gifts to me and to my parents, so that we can develop these gifts in Your timing and for Your glory, in Jesus' name. Amen.

Parental/Adult Engagement:
What are a few things that you do well and enjoy? How can you begin to develop your gifts?

Personal Notes/Personal Thoughts:

_____
_____
_____
_____
_____
_____
_____
_____
_____

Day 8
H
HELPFUL

Declaration: "I AM HELPFUL!"

Scriptures of Worth, Confidence and Character:
"Do to others as you would have them do to you." *Luke 6:31 NIV*

"Let each of you look out not only for his own interests, but also for the interests of others." *Philippians 2:4 NKJV*

Words of Worth, Confidence and Character:
You are helpful!

Do you know what it means to really be helpful? Well, the scriptures above give us some insight about how we can truly help others, like our family members, friends, teachers, church leaders or even our neighbors and community friends. Jesus gave some great advice that teaches us to treat others the same way that we would like to be treated. All of us can appreciate good help. Can you think of some ways that you could be helpful to others? Maybe you could wash the dishes, cut the grass, help with cooking, help clean the house, bring in groceries, pray for a friend, or even help your little sister or brother with a task that is difficult. On a larger scale, maybe you could start a food drive for the homeless in your city, wash your neighbor's car, donate your toys to children less fortunate or go on a mission trip for kids to serve others.

When I was younger, my grandfather got sick and there were many things that he was no longer able to do for himself. One simple thing he needed help with was putting lotion on his legs and feet. My siblings and I would take turns putting lotion on him, just because it was one task that we could help with. He appreciated even that small role that we were able to help with. There are lots of creative ways to help others and God has called you to be helpful and mindful of the wellbeing of others. Sometimes being helpful can be as basic as being respectful to the adults in your life and listening to their instructions. Maybe you could wash the clothes, serve at your church, or offer to help someone with their smaller children. It's easy to just focus on yourself and only be concerned about your own life, your own goals, and your own family. However, God has called us to higher thinking. He is developing character in you that is rooted in His love and serving others.

Prayer: Lord, I love You. Thank You for giving me the ability to help and serve others. Show me what I can do to help others and be a blessing to someone else. Give me the grace to treat others the way that I would like to be treated. I want to be more like You, in Jesus' name. Amen.

Parental/Adult Engagement:
What are some ways that you can be helpful to others?

Personal Notes/Personal Thoughts:

_____

_____

_____

_____

_____

_____

_____

_____

_____

Day 9
I
INTELLIGENT

Declaration: "I AM INTELLIGENT!"

Scriptures of Worth, Confidence and Character:
"As for these four young men, God gave them knowledge and skill in all literature and wisdom..." *Daniel 1:17a NKJV*

"And I have filled him with the Spirit of God, in wisdom, in understanding, in knowledge, and in all manner of workmanship." *Exodus 31:3 NKJV*

"I can do all things through Christ who strengthens me." *Phillipians 4:13 NKJV*

Words of Worth, Confidence and Character:
You are intelligent!

God has given you wisdom, knowledge, understanding and skill in various school subjects. God has given you a desire to learn, read, listen, grow, and study. This inward ability from God can help you with school, assignments, lessons, and any new material that comes your way. Just like He gave it to those mentioned in the scriptures above (Daniel and his friends), God has given it to you as well. When I was in second grade, my family moved to Shaker Heights, Ohio. I became the new kid in class and my teacher wasn't sure that I could do the advanced schoolwork that some students were doing in her class.

Even though I was doing accelerated schoolwork at my old school and participating in advanced placement for my grade level, she decided to place me in the 'lower' level group. Fortunately, my mom pushed for her to give me the more advanced schoolwork and the Lord allowed me to excel and do well. God was with me.

He helped me adjust to my new school, new schoolwork and blessed me as one of the smartest kids in my class. These younger years were important in building my self-confidence and I'm thankful to be able to look back and know that God's hand was on my life, even as a young person.

Right now, He is available to help you, too! All you need to do is ask Him for His help. It will require work and effort on your part. You will need to focus on your studies and eliminate distractions. You must concentrate on your assignments, even when you don't feel like it. You will need to focus and not make excuses. Know that God is with you and for you, regardless of whether you do homeschooling, virtual learning, or in-person learning. Perhaps, you have been labeled with ADHD, an IEP or some other learning disorder. The good news is that God is greater than any disorder and His grace is available to you, to help you overcome those challenges. His desire is to see you excel and do well, because you are intelligent, and you are His child.

Trust in His strength and ability to get you through any tough times you may be experiencing in school. YOU can do all things through Christ who strengthens YOU!

Prayer: Lord, I love You so much. I thank You for making me an intelligent person. You fill me with knowledge and skill for all my classes and studies. You care about my schoolwork and my ability to learn and do well. Thank You that I can do all things through Christ who strengthens me. I receive your knowledge, skill, and strength, in Jesus' name. Amen.

Parental/Adult Engagement:
What does this message on being *'intelligent'* mean to you? How can you apply it to your life?

Personal Notes/Personal Thoughts:

_____

_____

_____

_____

_____

_____

_____

_____

_____

_____

_____

_____

_____

_____

_____

_____

_____

_____

_____

_____

_____

_____

_____

_____

Day 10
J
JOYFUL

Declaration: "I AM JOYFUL!"

Scriptures of Worth, Confidence and Character:
"But the fruit of the Spirit is love, joy, peace, patience, kindness, goodness, faithfulness, gentleness, self-control. Against such there is no law." *Galatians 5:22,23 ESV*

"...do not sorrow, for the joy of the Lord is your strength." *Nehemiah 8:10*

"You will show me the path of life; In Your presence is fullness of joy; at Your right hand are pleasures forevermore." *Psalm 16:11 NKJV*

Words of Worth, Confidence and Character:
You are joyful!

Joy is a part of the fruit of the spirit. The fruit of the spirit are 9 different character traits (not really fruit that you eat). These 9 different character traits describe a person that has allowed God to shape their personality, emotions, and responses to everyday life events. Joy happens to be one character fruit. Just like apples grow on apple trees and peaches grow on peach trees, this character fruit can grow in your life, as one of God's trees *(Isaiah 61:3)*. God desires for you to have and experience joy because of Him. Joy comes from God's presence and goodness in your life, not from just 'getting what you want all the time'. Joy lifts you up, even when things can feel a little down. Joy is an inner strength. God's joy is a force that will help you overcome sadness, loneliness, depression, or difficult times. Joy feels very similar to happiness, but it is not based upon what's "happening" in your life. Joy is based upon knowing that God is with you, and that He is good, regardless of how things may look and feel at times. Joy is based upon knowing that He always wants the best for you. We live during a time when some kids are being challenged with depression, bad thoughts, and negative feelings. There are things that can happen to you, around you or even on the news, that can be traumatic or overwhelming at times.

I can remember feeling discouraged and disappointed one summer and even upset with my parents over how my summers were spent away from home as a kid. But the Lord was always with me, and He always covered and protected me. He taught me how to choose joy even in those times and to choose to have a good attitude. We all must learn to make the most of unpleasant situations, resist disappointments and choose joy. How do we do this? I'm glad you asked. His joy is in you. Your job is to cultivate it (make it grow) and release it into your life. This kind of joy comes from spending time in His Word and books that encourage your walk with God. This joy also comes from singing, praising, and worshiping God with those songs that help you feel God's presence. Joy comes from spending time with the Lord and other people that sincerely love Him. Here's something that may surprise you, my friend: Life is not perfect for adults or kids but please let these words from Jesus encourage you. "...In the world you will have tribulation (trouble, difficulties, disappointments), but be of good cheer, I have overcome the world" *(John 16:33 NKJV)*. The good news is, Jesus tells us to cheer up because He has already defeated everything that comes our way. So, cheer up my friend, regardless of how you feel and allow the joy of the Lord to be your strength today.

Prayer: Lord, I love You. Thank You for giving me Your joy. Your joy is my strength. I choose to walk in joy, regardless of what comes my way. I know that disappointments and challenges may come, but I choose to be of good cheer, because You have already overcome the world. You love me and You are for me, in Jesus' name, amen.

Parental/Adult Engagement:
Do you feel discouraged or disappointed about something?

How can you choose joy and make the most of an unpleasant situation?

Personal Notes/Personal Thoughts:

_____

_____

_____

_____

_____

_____

_____

_____

_____

_____

_____

_____

_____

_____

_____

_____

_____

Day 11
K
KIND

Scriptures of Worth, Confidence and Character:
"But the fruit of the Spirit is love, joy, peace, patience, kindness, goodness, faithfulness, gentleness and self-control. Against such there is no law." *Galatians 5: 22,23 NKJV*

"What is desired in a man is kindness..." *Proverbs 19:22 NKJV*

"Therefore, as the elect of God, holy and beloved, put on tender mercies, kindness, humility, meekness, long suffering..." *Colossians 3:12 NKJV*

Words of Worth, Confidence and Character:
You are kind!

Kindness is another fruit of the spirit. As we discussed before, apple trees grow apples, peach trees grow peaches, and as God's tree, you will grow His character fruit, known as the fruit of the spirit. When you have a relationship with the Lord, He puts these special qualities on the inside of you, like kindness. A kind person is someone that is friendly, generous, and considerate to others. Kindness reflects His love flowing through your life to others. I often must remind my daughters and my nieces to be kind to one another and others. It's so easy for them to fight over a toy, tease each other or even scream at one another. I want you to know that being mean to others, not sharing, bullying, name-calling, physical roughness, and the like can be seen in the life of many young people. But God has called you to be different. We live in a world where people have forgotten the importance of kindness. God has called you to be kind, even if someone disagrees with you. God has called you to be kind, even when someone believes differently from you. God has called you to be kind, even when someone looks differently than you; and God has even called you to be kind and forgive someone when they wrong you. This is the same kindness that Jesus showed us when He forgave us for our sins and died on the cross for us. He showed us amazing kindness when He didn't have to. In response to His great love for us, we should reflect His kindness to others even during the times when we don't want to. Being kind to others is an expression of His love. I challenge you to be kind to at least 3 people that come across your path this week. Maybe if we all did this, we could start a kindness revolution. Be kind and be bold with your kindness. In the midst of disagreements and differences, this world desperately needs a kindness revolution and maybe it can start with you.

Prayer: Lord, I love You. Thank You for helping me to walk in kindness and extend your love to my parents, my siblings, my classmates, and all those I meet. I can be kind because You have put Your kindness on the inside in me, in Jesus' name. Amen.

Parental/Adult Engagement:
What are some ways that you can show kindness to others at school and at home? Will you accept the challenge to be kind to at least 3 people this week?

Personal Notes/Personal Thoughts:
_____
_____
_____
_____

Day 12
L
LOVED

Declaration: "I AM LOVED!"

Scriptures of Worth, Confidence and Character:
"For God so loved the world that He gave His
only begotten Son, that whoever believes in Him
should not perish but have everlasting life."
John 3:16 NKJV

Words of Worth, Confidence and Character:
You are loved!

God dearly loved you even before you were born. While you were still inside of your mom's belly, He was thinking about you and looking forward to the great plans He would have in store for your future. I remember being pregnant with each one of my girls, Grace, Charis, and Hannah. My husband and I planned big things for their arrival. We painted the room, bought cute little furniture, and decorated with fun toys and stuffed animals. We purchased a new SUV so that we would have enough room for the little ones and their car seats. We were prepared to give them everything they needed to be happy, healthy, and successful in life. Yet, even as human parents that loved our girls deeply, and wanted to prepare special things for their arrival, our love could not compare to God's amazing love. Similarly, God's love for you is so much bigger than what your parents can buy for you and so much greater than what people can do for you.

God's love for you is bigger, greater, wider, and deeper than you will ever know. Of course, He cares about the food you eat, the clothes you wear, your school experiences and everyday life, but He deeply cares about your relationship with Him. Now, that you are growing up in so many ways, He still wants you to know how much He deeply cares about you. He sent His Son Jesus to die on a cross for your sins, to be your personal Savior and hero. We all make mistakes, but nothing that you have done or will ever do, can separate you from His love. No mistake, no failure, no bad decision can separate you from His love. His arms of love and forgiveness are always open for you. He sent His Son, Jesus to rescue you from your sins. By doing this, He has given you eternal life, which means you get to live with God forever. In other words, you get to spend "forever" with this amazing God and enjoy the benefits of His goodness and mercy.

He has made you a part of His family, through the sacrifice of His Son. All you need to do is receive His love and accept the special sacrifice of His Son, Jesus. There is no greater love than His love. My friend, always know that you are dearly loved by the God of the universe and that His love is the greatest love of all.

Prayer: Lord, I love You and I thank You for loving me. I receive Your amazing love. Help me to understand this great love that You have for me and help me to respond by giving my life to Jesus. My response to Your love is the surrender of my heart to You, in Jesus' name. Amen.

Parental/Adult Engagement:
Did you know that God loves you so much that He sent His Son, Jesus, to be your Lord and Savior?

Personal Notes/Personal Thoughts:

Day 13
M
MARVELOUS

Declaration: "I AM MARVELOUS!"

Scriptures of Worth, Confidence and Character:
"I will praise You for I am fearfully and wonderfully made; Marvelous are Your works, and that my soul knows very well." *Psalms 139:14 NKJV*

"For we are God's masterpiece. He has created us anew in Christ Jesus, so we can do the good things He planned for us long ago." *Ephesian 2:10 NLT*

Words of Worth, Confidence and Character:
You are marvelous!

The writer of *Psalms 139* is describing the magnificence and greatness of realizing that he is a hand-made, carefully crafted, personal artwork of the Almighty God. Guess what? So, are you! You are a hand-made, carefully crafted, personal artwork of our awesome and amazing God. Every single bone, organ, muscle, and body part that makes up your human body is a part of God's spectacular design. Your eyes are a gift from God that provide sight. Your nose is a gift from God that allows the ability to smell. Your ears are a gift from God that provide the ability to hear. Your tongue is a gift from God that allows you to taste and enjoy your food. Your fingerprints are so special that no one else in the world has the same fingerprints as you. Your skin is a special gift from God. It provides protection from the environment, regulates body temperature, and provides the sensation of touch.

Please understand, your skin is beautiful, made by God and comes in all different shades of black, brown, tan, peach, and shades in between. Your unique voice is a gift from God that allows you to speak, sing, laugh and pray. My friend, your personality, hair texture, smile and sense of humor make you "one of a kind", a masterpiece! God invested time and care to make you into the masterpiece that you are. There is no one else just like MARVELOUS, YOU! I want you to become your #1 fan! Love yourself! Build your confidence and worth on this truth and you will never compare yourself with anyone else. When I was younger, I used to look at another person's hair, clothes, skin color, and personality wondering if they were better than me. I appeared confident on the outside, but I struggled with doubts about myself on the inside. It wasn't until I developed a real relationship with the Lord, for myself, that I realized these scriptures, like the ones I shared, actually applied to me too. It changed my life to understand that God personally made me, loved me, and called me 'marvelous". I want you to be confident in who He has created you to be, too. I teach my girls to love their beautiful brown skin and their beautifully textured curls and braids because they are also gifts from God.

My friend, please don't compare yourself with anyone at school, on social media, YouTube, television, or a magazine. God didn't create you for comparison, He created you for His unique purpose and His love. Receive His love and in response, be confident and love yourself as the masterpiece that God has created you to be.

Prayer: Lord, I love You! Now I understand what it means for me to know that I am marvelous. I am marvelous because You made me, You love me and You hand-crafted me as Your very own. I will build my self-esteem around this truth. I am fearfully and wonderfully made. I love ME, because You are teaching me to love me, in Jesus' name. Amen.

Parental/Adult Engagement:
As God's masterpiece, what are some things that make you *'marvelous'*?

Personal Notes/Personal Thoughts:

_____

_____

_____

_____

_____

_____

_____

_____

_____

_____

_____

_____

_____

_____

_____

_____

_____

_____

_____

_____

_____

_____

Day 14
N
NICE

Declaration: "I AM NICE!"

Scriptures of Worth, Confidence and Character:
"Therefore, as we have opportunity let us do good to all, especially to those who are of the household of faith." *Galatians 6:10 NKJV*

Words of Worth, Confidence and Character:
You are nice!

The passage above reminds us that opportunities to do good things will happen all throughout life and even throughout our day. You will have an opportunity to clean up without being asked, share your things, help your grandparents, serve your community, pray for a friend, or give to someone in need. These opportunities, or moments to do good and be nice will happen when we least expect it. If your mom is anything like me, she is often telling you, "Be nice." I say it to my kids all the time, throughout their day, as I want them to be mindful of their interactions with one another and others. Simply being nice and respectful is the beginning of 'doing good to all', regardless of the other person's age, gender, skin color, culture, beliefs, or differences. As a young black girl, I grew up in a diverse community and had friends from many different racial backgrounds. We went to school together, had our play dates and enjoyed fun activities together with our Girl Scouts troop.

Although we were all different, we were all friends. It may seem strange for me to say that 'we were all different, yet we were all friends', because right now we live during a time of racial tension. Unfortunately, some people have not been properly taught that all people (of all skin colors and backgrounds) have been made in the image and likeness of God. This is a sad truth. But God values all people and loves each one dearly. God will make sure that you have opportunities to be nice and do good to people who look like you, as well as people who don't look like you. It is important that you recognize this opportunity, so that the love of God can flow through you as a young person. You can be an instrument of hope and racial healing. You are an extension of Him, so being nice to others reflects His goodness. When people interact with you and experience how nice you are to them, it pleases God's heart and releases His love. Look for opportunities to do good because they are actually all around you.

Prayer: Lord, I love You. Thank You for helping me to be nice. Please help me to be nice to my parents, siblings, and family members, and even to others who don't look like me or talk like me. Help me to be nice, do good and show kindness to people that are different from me. All people are created in Your image and Your likeness. Help me to represent You well, in Jesus' name. Amen.

Parental/Adult Engagement:
Do you have opportunities to be nice and to do good to others?

Personal Notes/Personal Thoughts:

_____

_____

_____

_____

_____

_____

Day 15
O
OUTSTANDING

Declaration: "I AM OUTSTANDING!"

Scriptures of Worth, Confidence and Character:
"But the Lord said to Samuel, 'Do not look at his appearance or at his physical stature, because I have refused him. For the Lord does not see as man sees; for man looks at the outward appearance, but the Lord looks at the heart.'" *1 Samuel 16:7 NKJV*

"But the Lord said to Samuel, 'Pay no attention to how tall and handsome he is. I have rejected him because I do not judge as people judge. They look at the outward appearance, but I look at the heart.'" *1 Samuel 16:7 GNB*

Words of Worth, Confidence and Character:
You are outstanding!

The word outstanding means to be exceptionally good. It also means to stand out from the rest. This passage of scripture is very important to the life of King David because this scripture describes his life as a young person before he was ever anointed as King. The prophet Samuel had the job of finding the new king of Israel, recognizing him, and announcing that he would be the future leader. Well, most people however, think of a king as someone tall, strong, handsome, and regal; someone who 'looks like a king'. God wasn't interested in his "looks". God was interested in his "heart" and "attitude". David was an outstanding young man because he had a pure heart, and he loved God with all his heart. He was a young shepherd that was faithful over his flock and faithful in worshiping the Lord, even when no one was watching him. His heart of love, obedience, faithfulness, and worship caused him to be chosen as King, even over his older, more qualified brothers. I want to highlight something about this scripture. Personal appearance is important but not the most important thing. You should take good care of yourself. Personal hygiene is important. Brush your teeth, eat healthy foods, get proper exercise, and take care of your body because it is God's temple. There is nothing wrong with wanting to look nice, dress well, be fashionable and present yourself in an attractive yet appropriate manner. However, your outward appearance or "looks" are never more important than your inner attitude, emotions, and thoughts. Unfortunately, many people would rather 'look good' on the outside than 'look good to God' on the inside.

God sees the things that other people cannot see. God saw David faithfully taking care of his flock, and God also sees you faithfully doing those tasks that you have been asked to do. A person of good character will do what is right, even when no one else is watching them. When no one else is watching, God is always watching. He can see the thoughts, emotions and attitudes of our heart, and He is carefully watching over our lives to help us develop outstanding character and transformed hearts. Like young David, who went on to do great things throughout his life, you too are a young person that is called to do great things in life. Even now, God is transforming your heart and preparing you for the amazing things He has chosen for you.

Prayer: Lord, I love You. Thank you for seeing my heart. Create in me a clean heart and continue to build outstanding character in me. Man looks on the outside, but You look on the inside. Help me to take very good care of my personal hygiene and appearance but, even more, to focus on pleasing You with my entire life, in Jesus' name. Amen

Parental/Adult Engagement:
What does this message about being *'outstanding'* mean to you? Your "looks" are never more important than your attitude, emotions, and thoughts. What does this mean to you?

Personal Notes/Personal Thoughts:

_____

_____

_____

_____

_____

_____

_____

_____

_____

_____

_____

_____

_____

_____

_____

_____

_____

_____

_____

_____

_____

Day 16
P
PRECIOUS

Declaration: "I AM PRECIOUS!"

Scriptures of Worth, Confidence and Character:
"Because you are precious in My eyes, and honored,
and I love you, I give men in return for you, people
in exchange for your life." *Isaiah 43:4 ESV*

"How precious also are your thoughts toward me, O God!
How great is the sum of them!" *Psalms 139:17 NKJV*

Words of Worth, Confidence and Character:
You are precious!

You are of great value to God and to those who love
you. Your life is special, and God deeply cares for you.
Let that sink in for a moment. God deeply cares for you
and deeply loves you. He inspired me to write this very
book so that you would read these words at this very
moment. You are important to God and your life, even at
your age, matters very much to His plan and purpose.
You may not feel precious to Him when your parents are
having challenges or when your grandparent is sick or
when you must move to a new school. Family issues,
school issues and relationship issues can also make you
question God's love and concern. No matter what life
brings, always know He has precious thoughts that He
is thinking all the time about you. You are His precious
one, and the same way I think about my kids, God thinks
about you (His kid). As a parent, I would give anything
for my girls, and my desire is to see them consistently
walking in God's plan for their lives. My girls can come

to me with anything, good or bad. I'm here for them, no matter what.

As your Heavenly Parent, God feels the exact same way about you. So, that means God is a safe place where you can bring any worries, problems, fears, or emotions because He cares, and He is concerned about everything in your life. And that, my friend, is what it means to be precious to God.

Prayer: I love You, Lord! Thank You for valuing my life. I choose to find my worth and value within Your Word and my relationship with You. Your Word says that I am precious in Your sight and so I receive Your love and the precious thoughts You are thinking about me. Let Your will be done in my life, in Jesus' name. Amen.

Parental/Adult Engagement:
Do you understand that God is concerned about every area of your life because you are precious to Him? What problems or fears do you need to bring to God?

Personal Notes/Personal Thoughts:

_____

_____

_____

_____

_____

_____

_____

_____

_____

_____

_____

_____

Day 17
Q
QUITE CLEVER

Declaration: "I AM QUITE CLEVER!"

Scriptures of Worth, Confidence and Character:
"For the Lord gives wisdom; from His mouth come knowledge and understanding. He stores up sound wisdom for the upright;" *Proverbs 2:6,7a NKJV*

Words of Worth, Confidence and Character:
You are quite clever!

The word clever is a fancy word for being smart, wise, or skillful. The Lord is the One who gives you wisdom, knowledge and understanding about everything in your life. His wisdom and cleverness will lead and guide you to make good decisions, even as a young person. However, it is something that we need to develop, and grow in. I clearly remember one day in the first grade, when I decided to walk home from school, instead of returning home on the school bus. Riding the school bus home was my usual plan. However, I decided to walk home, without even asking my parents. I thought I was big enough to walk home alone and that everything would be just fine. Well, this was a not-so-good decision on my part.

My mom was scared and worried when she didn't see me get off the bus that day. I was still walking home and hoping that I remembered how to get there all by myself. I was only about 6 or 7 years old at the time and my mom feared that something terrible had happened to me when I didn't get off at my bus stop. Fortunately, the Lord protected me during my long walk home and I eventually made it home. My mom was waiting for me with my grandfather (who kept her from spanking me). I learned a big lesson that day about using wisdom, being clever, making good decisions and obeying my parents. I am grateful that I got home safely.

We live in a world where it is important for young people to be safe, communicate with their parents about where they are and remember "stranger-danger". Your parents, teachers and other adults may have certain rules and guidelines in place to help keep you safe and protected as a young person. It is always a clever and wise choice to work with these important adults in your life, as they are assisting you during your life's journey. Now that I am a mom, I totally understand why my mom got so upset with me that day. These adults care for you. These adults are gifts from God to help you make good decisions. Please know, God will give you wisdom from His Word to help you with school, family issues, your behavior, or anything that comes up in your life. Many times, that cleverness will come in the form of instructions from your parents, teachers, and pastors.

Prayer: Lord, I love You! Thank You for giving me wisdom, insight, and direction during my life's journey. I am quite clever because of Your leading and guiding and the wisdom that comes from the adults in my life. I will continue to learn more about You and read Your Word so that I can grow in wisdom and stature and in favor with God and men, just like Jesus. In Jesus' name, I pray. Amen.

Parental/Adult Engagement:
What does this lesson mean to you? How can you apply it to your life at this time?

Personal Notes/Personal Thoughts:

Day 18
R
RARE

Declaration "I AM RARE!"

Scriptures of Worth, Confidence and Character:
"Before I formed you in the womb, I knew you; Before you were born, I sanctified you..." *Jeremiah 1:5a NKJV*

"For You formed my inward parts; You covered me in my mother's womb." *Psalm 139:13 NKJV*

Words of Worth, Confidence and Character:
You are rare!

When I was growing up, my dad had an interesting hobby; he collected corvettes. Corvettes are fast, two-door, two person sports cars, and he used them for racing and car shows. Everyone admired his corvettes because he had a few rare cars; limited edition cars. Corvettes have been around for over 60 years and many people really like these cars. These corvettes were different from all other cars and in a very special category of their own because of their cool colors, sporty design, powerful engine, and speed. All my friends loved his corvettes, and even random people would complement my dad on his cool corvettes. Like one of my dad's corvettes, you are a rare and very interesting person. God designed you and there is no one else who is just like YOU. Not to be compared with anyone else, you are also in a special category of your own. Your smile, your personality, your style, your likes, your laugh, and your experiences altogether make you the rare young person that brings a smile to the heart of God.

Before you were born, God knew you and loved you. He formed your hands and feet, your eyes and ears and made you into the amazing YOU that we see today. No, you aren't perfect and yes, you will make mistakes. We all make mistakes. But that doesn't change the fact that God has always had big plans in store for you from the very beginning. You are very special to God and it's not based on 'what you do', but 'who you are'. You are His! Begin to realize this and embrace it. Treasure and love yourself as He already does. Yes, He created you for great things even before you were born. Think about that. Wow, right?!

Prayer: Lord, I love You! Thank You for showing me how rare and special I am. I'm not average or ordinary, but I am rare, unique, and special. You made me, You love me and I choose to love myself and accept all the unique things that make me, me.

Parental/Adult Engagement:
From your personality and likes, to your life experiences, what makes you a rare and interesting person?

Personal Notes/Personal Thoughts:

_____

_____

_____

_____

_____

_____

_____

_____

_____

_____

_____

_____

Day 19
S
SPECIAL

Declaration: "I AM SPECIAL!"

Scriptures of Worth, Confidence and Character:
"But you are a chosen generation, a royal priesthood,
a holy nation, His own special people, that you may
proclaim the praises of Him who called you out of
darkness into His marvelous light;" *1Peter 2:9 NKJV*

"For you are a holy people to the Lord your God; the
Lord your God has chosen you to be a people for
Himself, a special treasure above all the peoples on
the face of the earth." *Deuteronomy 7:6 NKJV*

Words of Worth, Confidence and Character:
You are special!

God calls you His special treasure, which means you
are of great worth and value to God. You are very
important to Him. So, you should never allow someone
to make you feel 'less than' special or 'less than' valued.
Begin to see yourself the very same way that God sees
you. From your hair texture, skin color, unique talents,
awesome personality, and style, you are one-of-a-kind,
hand-made by the Lord. Your academic strengths,
creative abilities, and athletic gifts may set you apart
but always know that God loves you for 'who you are',
not for 'what you do'. There was a time when I looked at
others and wanted to dress like them or have the same
kind of hair. I wanted a certain group of people to like me
at school. I wanted to be good at gymnastics like one of
my friends.

As a kid, I remember being envious of others. I wanted what they had, without fully recognizing how God blessed me and how God made me special. As a kid, I didn't fully know that I was special to God or that He loved me and called me His very own. I found my identity in my athletic ability, academic success, and extracurricular activities. My identity and self-worth were connected to these things rather than God, so I always had some self-doubt about my worth and value. Was I good enough? Was I smart enough? Was I pretty enough? These questions and more would come to my mind from time to time.

Maybe you have similar questions that come to you, as a young person. I want you to know that God loves you and that you are His "...special treasure above all the people on the face of the earth". His love and His grace will always be ENOUGH for the questions that come to your mind. Remember that God has called you, His chosen generation, and He chose you on purpose. So, give Him all your doubts and questions, just like I did, because He has hand-picked you to be special for His glory.

Prayer: Dear Lord, I love You. Thank You for making me Your special treasure. I receive Your love for me, and I will never be the same, in Jesus' name. Amen.

Parental/Adult Engagement:
We all have moment of self-doubt, but do you realize how special YOU are to the Lord?

Personal Notes/Personal Thoughts:

_____

_____

_____

_____

Day 20
T
TALENTED

Declaration: "I AM TALENTED!"

Scriptures of Worth, Confidence and Character:
"For the kingdom of heaven is like a man traveling to a far country, who called his own servants and delivered his goods to them. And to one he gave five talents, to another two talents and to another one, to each according to his own ability; and immediately he went on a journey. Then he who had received five talents went and traded with them and made another five talents. And likewise, he who had received two gained two more also. But he who had received one went and dug in the ground and hid his lord's money. After a long time the lord of those servants came and settled accounts with them." *Matthew 25: 14-19 NKJV*

Words of Worth, Confidence and Character:
You are talented.

In the passage above, we see a story describing 'talents' that were given to 3 different people. In this passage of scripture, those "talents" are referring to money that was given to each person, but I like the use of the word, talent because this story is a great example of how you should use your gifts and talents wisely. God wants you to enjoy, explore and maximize your talents. Discover your talents, strengths, and gifts and recognize some of the great stuff that God has put on the inside of you. My husband, Gareth is one of those people that has multiple talents. He grew up playing the drums in his church, and later became a percussionist (drum section) in his school marching band. Growing up he could have played any sport but was really good at playing football. He went on to play during all his school years and even into college.

He also participated in student government in school and was considered a true leader amongst his classmates. He was recognized for his excellent schoolwork and academic achievements. So, here is my challenge for you- Don't waste your skills. Don't shy away from your greatness. Be bold. Be great. Be yourself. Be the YOU that God has created and ordained you to be, as you identify your own unique skills that come from Him. Athletic abilities, academic abilities, musical abilities, scientific abilities, artistic abilities, serving abilities and all talents come from Him. Don't hide your talent from the world around you, just because your talent doesn't look like or sound like someone else's talent.

Be YOU. Be courageous enough to allow your talents to bless the world and glorify God in your own special way. This generation needs your talents!

Prayer: Lord, I love You. Thank You for the talents You have given me. I will not bury them or hide them, but I will embrace them and celebrate who You have create me to be and allow my talents to honor You, in Jesus' name, amen.

Parental/Adult Engagement:
What are some of your talents or abilities?

Personal Notes/Personal Thoughts:

_____

_____

_____

_____

_____

_____

_____

Day 21
U
UNIQUE

Declaration: "I AM UNIQUE!"

Scriptures of Worth, Confidence and Character:
"And He has made from one blood every nation of men to dwell on all the face of the earth, and has determined their pre-appointed times and the boundaries of their dwellings..." *Acts 17:26 NKJV*

"After this I looked, and there was an enormous crowd- no one could count all the people! They were from every race, tribe, nation, and language and they stood in front of the throne and of the Lamb, dressed in white robes and holding palm branches in their hands. They called out in a loud voice: 'Salvation comes from our God, who sits on the throne, and from the Lamb!'" *Revelation 7:9,10 GNB*

Words of Worth, Confidence and Character:
You are unique.

God wants you to embrace and celebrate your uniqueness. In other words, God wants you to be proud of those things that make you different and special. God is the one that has created every ethnicity, every skin color, every language, and every nation and assigned them to every human being. God has blessed you with your own special cultural uniqueness. You don't have to compare yourself with others or want to be like them. God wants you to love yourself and all the things that make you, YOU! Your family and your family traditions make you unique. Being the oldest, middle, or even the youngest child in your family makes you, unique. Wearing glasses, having military parents or living with your grandparents are all examples of interesting things that make you unique. Maybe you are being raised by a great single mom and that makes you unique. Maybe you have a parent that has passed away, yet God has uniquely brought other people into your life to care for you. Maybe you have had some health challenges, but God is helping you work through all those challenges. (Romans 8:28). God already knew your birthday, your parents, your hair color, eye color, gender, city, state and country of birth long before you ever arrived.

All the things that make you unique, special, and set apart are the very things He loves about you and the very things that tell your amazing story to the world. These things become a part of your testimony. Your life is proof to others that God is a good God. God loves you and He decided for you to be born, for this very time in history. This world needs someone that is unique, like you, to represent Jesus in a loving way. God is counting on you, to be your very best self and to be uniquely, you, for His glory and His purpose for your life. Embrace this as young person, so that as you grow and mature, you won't need to compare or compete with others. You will be fully confident in the person that He has called and created you to be.

Prayer: Lord, I love You. I embrace my uniqueness and I celebrate all the things that make me different and special. You have given me my language, eye color, hair texture, skin color, family, birthday, and all of these cool things that make me, ME. Help me to love me and receive your love for me and be my best self for your glory, in Jesus' name. Amen.

Parental/Adult Engagement:
What are some things that make you unique?

Personal Notes/Personal Thoughts:

Day 22
V
VERY POLITE

Declaration: "I AM VERY POLITE!"

Scriptures of Worth, Confidence and Character:
"There is a saying, 'Love your friends and hate your
enemies.' But I say: Love your enemies! Pray for those
who persecute you! In that way you will be acting as true
sons of your Father in heaven. *Matthew 5:43-45 NKJV*

Words of Worth, Confidence and Character:
You are very polite.

That simply means that you are respectful and
considerate of other people. We live during a time when
being a polite person is rare. Bullying is a problem
in school between students and it is also a problem
within our society. It is a fact of life that some people
will be mean to others. We cannot control the behavior
of others, but we can control how we respond to their
behavior. I can remember seeing other kids get teased
in school for different reasons, but I never really knew
how to stand up for them or how to help them. At the
very least I should have told an adult, like a teacher or
even the principal, but I feared being labeled a "snitch".
In other words, I didn't want them to start bullying me
too. God has a greater plan for you and me. We live by
a higher standard. God has called us to pray for those
who bully others, and to pray for those who are hateful
and mean to others. God has called you to pray for even
those who are hurtful and mean to you, as well.

Like Jesus explains in the scripture, most people can easily be polite and kind to those who are their friends, but to show kindness and be polite toward those who are mean to you, requires a special understanding. When you love your enemies, you make God smile. When you love your enemies, by praying for them, you are living out a God-kind-of-love that is greater than any form of hate, persecution, racism, or bullying. This kind of politeness, kindness and love is revolutionary, which means it can change a person's heart. This kind of politeness, kindness and love can change the world, one person at a time. Never underestimate God's power that flows through your politeness, kindness, and love towards those who do not seem to deserve it in our eyes. Let God use you in this important way.

Prayer: I love You, Lord. Help me to love my enemies and to pray for those who bullying others and are mean. In doing this, I am representing You, and being the polite, considerate person, You have called me to be, in Jesus' name. Amen.

Parental/Adult Engagement:
Have you ever experienced bullying?
Is there someone that you can pray for at this time?
Have you ever discussed bullying with an adult?

Personal Notes/Personal Thoughts:

_____

_____

_____

_____

_____

_____

_____

_____

Day 23
W
WONDERFUL

Declaration: "I AM WONDERFUL!"

Scriptures of Worth, Confidence and Character:
"O Lord, You are my God. I will exalt You, I will praise Your name, for You have done wonderful things; Your counsels of old are faithfulness and truth." *Isaiah 25:1 NKJV*

"For unto us a Child is born, unto us a Son is given; And the government will be upon His shoulder. And His name will be called, Wonderful, Counselor, Mighty God, Everlasting Father, Prince of Peace." *Isaiah 9:6 NKJV*

"We will not keep them from our children; we will tell the next generation about the Lord's power and his great deeds and the wonderful things He has done." *Psalm 78:4 NKJV*

Words of Worth, Confidence and Character:
You are wonderful!

The scriptures tell us about the wonderful things God has done and YOU are one of those wonderful things that He has done. The scripture also tells us that He is also called, Wonderful Counselor. God, who is wonderful, has already prepared some wonderful counsel or advice for you. God knew that you would need help, living this life and growing into the amazing person He has created you to be, so He has given you parents, pastors, teachers, mentors, and others to provide wisdom, guidance and insight for anything you might face. Growing up can have its various challenges but nothing is too hard for God and His Word. Answers are always waiting for you, through the wonderful counsel of God's Word, the Bible. Even through devotionals like these, He wants you to learn His voice, understand more about His ways, read your bible, and get to know Him for yourself. I was inspired to write this book because I wanted my 3 daughters to have a book like this to encourage them to build their self-worth and self-confidence around the wonderful Word of God.

I went to church as a kid with my family, but I didn't take time to get to know God for myself. I didn't realize that He really cared about the details of my young life until I was much older. Please know, that right now as a young person, you have a special opportunity to get to know God, as His friend. It's my responsibility to let you (the next generation) know about the Lord's power and His great deeds and the wonderful things He has done. The scriptures show us David defeating Goliath *(1 Samuel 17:1-50 NKJV)*, Daniel escaping the mouths of lions *(Daniel 6:16-23 NKJV)* and three Hebrews boys that were protected from a fiery furnace *(Daniel 3:8-30 NKJV)*. These are all great bible miracles that detail the wonderful things that God has done.

Just think, there is a wonderful story to be told through your life too, even if you can't see it yet. Regardless of the hurt, confusion, mistreatment, or disappointments you may have experienced at different times, don't ever feel like you must face things alone or that someone else wouldn't be able to understand how you feel. God loves you and His arms of love are always extended toward you. My challenge for you is to keep growing in your relationship with God so that you too can experience '... the Lord's power and His great deeds and the wonderful things He has done...' in your own life.

Prayer: I love You, Lord. I am wonderfully made by You, a Wonderful Counselor and You have prepared a wonderful life for me. Help me to lean on You and Your Word and the people You have placed in my life to help lead me on Your righteous path, in Jesus' name. Amen.

Parental/Adult Engagement:
What are some wonderful things that God has already done for you? What wonderful things do you see in your future?

Personal Notes/Personal Thoughts:

_____

_____

_____

_____

_____

_____

_____

_____

_____

_____

_____

_____

_____

_____

_____

_____

_____

_____

_____

_____

_____

_____

Day 24
X
EXQUISITE

Declaration: "I AM EXQUISITE!"

Scriptures of Worth, Confidence and Character:
"…Esther was brought to King Xerxes in the royal palace. The king liked her more than any of the other women, and more than any of the others she won his favor and affection. He placed the royal crown on her head and made her queen in place of Vashti. Then the king gave a great banquet in Esther's honor and invited all his officials and administrators. He proclaimed a holiday for the entire empire and distributed gifts worthy of a king."
Esther 2:16b-18 GNB

"One of his attendants said, 'Jesse, of the town of Bethlehem, has a son who is a good musician, He is also a brave and handsome man, a good soldier and an able speaker. The Lord is with him.'" *1Samuel 16:18 GNB*

Words of Worth, Confidence and Character:
You are exquisite!

The word exquisite describes someone who is extremely beautiful. In the case of a young man, it would describe someone who is very handsome. In the Bible, David is described as a very handsome young man and Esther is described as a very beautiful young woman. David is destined to become the king of Israel and Esther is destined to become Queen over the empire of her time, as well. However, if we take a deeper look into both of their personal lives, we discover that their outward beauty reflected their inner beauty and character. Both Esther and David had a special and specific calling to become royalty and to use their royal power for godly purposes. Like Queen Esther and King David, you also have a special and specific calling to be in God's family and to represent his kingdom on earth, as His chosen generation, a royal priesthood, and holy nation *(1 Peter 2:9)*. Like Queen Esther and King David, you must also understand that God has made you the very attractive person that you are on the outside, but He is more concerned that you become a person of confidence and character on the inside. Displaying a good attitude, having a pure heart, walking in humility, honesty, kindness, and love will always show a good representation of the kingdom of God. Throughout your life, God will give you special opportunities and open special doors for you, even as a young person. Always remember that your moments to shine become moments for others to experience getting to know a little more about God and His kingdom, through you. Maybe one day you will be the captain of your team, the president of your class, the leader of your band or the organizer of your community service event. Just like Esther and David, God has blessed you to be a blessing in your family, your community, your school, and your generation. Queen Esther is famous for courageously approaching the King and ultimately saving the Jewish people from being destroyed.

King David is famous for defeating Goliath the giant and ruling as a great king that pleased the Lord. How will you use your royal status in God's kingdom to positively impact those around you? You are God's royal representative to others. Always remember, your outward appearance should be coupled with character, confidence, and a desire to please the Lord.

Prayer: Lord, I love You. You created me and I am Yours. Help me to be the person of worth, confidence and character on the inside so that I can please you with my life, like Queen Esther and King David, in Jesus' name. Amen.

Parental/Adult Engagement:
What does today's lesson mean to you? How can you apply it to your own life?

Personal Notes/Personal Thoughts:

_____
_____
_____
_____
_____
_____
_____
_____
_____
_____
_____
_____
_____
_____
_____
_____
_____
_____
_____
_____
_____
_____
_____

Day 25
Y
EXTRAORDINARY

Declaration: "I AM EXTRAORDINARY!"

Scriptures of Worth, Confidence and Character:
"Do not let anyone look down on you because you are young but be an example for the believers in your speech, your conduct, your love, faith and purity." *1 Timothy 4:12 GNB*

Words of Worth, Confidence and Character:
You are extraordinary!

The word extraordinary is the combination of two words: extra and ordinary. The word extraordinary describes someone that is always "extra". This person is extra helpful, extra nice, extra special, extra kind, extra loving, extra amazing, extra talented, and more. An extraordinary person goes above and beyond what ordinary, regular people do in any given situation. You, my friend, are one of those extraordinary people. In the scripture above, the Apostle Paul wrote a letter to his young friend Timothy. Timothy was an extraordinary young person, like you. He loved God and he had great potential to do amazing things in his life. Paul wrote these words to his young friend, Timothy because he wanted him to understand that even young people should strive to set an example for others to follow. Because he understood that young people are leaders too, the Apostle Paul described several ways for young people to represent God in an extraordinary way. Other young people, and even adults, are watching your life: the words you speak, the life you live, your service to others, your behavior toward siblings, respect for your parents, your love for God and the purity of your life. This generation needs to see great examples everywhere. Schools, sports teams, churches, communities, and organizations are all looking for extraordinary people.

Are you willing to be an extraordinary example for others? It may just require you doing something 'extra', like taking out the trash without being asked or praying for a friend in need. An extraordinary person will protect their eyes, instead of watching something inappropriate on the internet, even though their friend decides to watch it.

An extraordinary person will be honest with their parents from now on. Being extraordinary means that you respect yourself, love yourself and do not accept disrespect, name-calling, bullying or any other questionable behavior from others. Being extraordinary means that you use your words to support and encourage others, because mean language discourages and harms people. Being extraordinary means walking in purity, having safe boundaries in all relationships, and building your self-confidence with the Word of God. People are watching you every day, including the people in your own family.

So, you have a great opportunity to be extraordinary every day. The challenge is yours, but God has already chosen you for this special assignment. He is with you, always, to give you the strength you need to live this out.

Prayer: Lord, I love You. Help me to be extraordinary for You, and to be an example for other young people to follow. Help me to be an example with my words, my lifestyle, my love for others, my faith in You, and a life of purity. Thank You for Your grace on my life to do these things, in Jesus' name. Amen.

Parental/Adult Engagement:
What is something "extra" that you can do, as an extraordinary person?

Personal Notes/Personal Thoughts:

_____

_____

_____

_____

_____

_____

_____

_____

_____

_____

_____

_____

_____

_____

_____

_____

_____

_____

_____

_____

_____

_____

_____

_____

_____

_____

_____

Day 26
Z
AMAZING

Declaration: "I AM AMAZING!"

Scriptures of Worth, Confidence and Character:
"When He came in, He said to them, 'Why make this commotion and weep? The child is not dead, but sleeping.' And they ridiculed Him. But when He had put them all outside, He took the father and the mother of the child, and those who were with Him, and entered where the child was lying. Then He took the child by the hand, and said to her, 'Talitha, cumi,' which is translated, 'Little girl, I say to you, arise'. Immediately, the girl arose and walked, for she was twelve years of age. And they were overcome with great amazement." *Mark 5:39-42 NKJV*

Words of Worth, Confidence and Character:
You are amazing!

The scripture you just read describes the moment that Jesus restored life back to a young twelve-year-old girl. It was a miracle. Jesus brought her back to life. There are so many great stories about the wonderful things that Jesus did for people while He walked on Earth. This story, however, is especially great because the person experiencing the miracle is a young person. God is ready to do miracles for YOU, not just the adults in your life. In school, I remember having a relationship that caused me to be brokenhearted and sad. During my sadness, I drew closer to the Lord and decided to really develop my friendship with God. This was something new for me, because until then, I saw God as more of a religion, rather than a God wanting a personal relationship with me. God truly comforted me during this time in my life, even when my parents could not, and His love was my miracle. His love for me as a young person, began the love I have for Him, even now. My personal journey of walking with Him every day began for me, as a young person. Like the scripture describes about the girl, I felt like the Lord "took me by the hand" and brought me back to life, rescuing me from my personal emptiness. That was my miracle.

I love how the scripture says that they were 'overcome with great amazement'. God used the life of this young person to display His goodness and power. As your life unfolds and you walk with the Lord, He will continue to do great things for you. You will experience your very own, personal miracles. Those who know you will be amazed by God and His great work in your life. You are amazing because He has created You in His image and for His purpose, to do amazing things. Maybe YOU will serve the homeless, bring healing to those who are hurting or become an inspiration for the next generation.

Maybe YOU will become a great peacemaker and bring hope to our communities. Perhaps, you will be an amazing president, an amazing scientist, an amazing preacher, an amazing teacher, or an amazing musician. God may use you to bring a refreshing change to your school or perhaps your family. Regardless of your age, I know from personal experience that God wants to do miracles in your life right now. God wants you to be 'overcome with great amazement' as you watch His great plans unfold for your life.

Prayer: Dear Lord, I love You. Thank You for Your amazing grace and love that transforms me into the amazing person You have called me to be. I welcome the miracles, signs and wonders that You want to perform in my life. Have Your way in my life, even as a young person, in Jesus' name. Amen.

Parental/Adult Engagement:
What amazing things would you like to see God do in your future?

Personal Notes/Personal Thoughts:

_____

_____

_____

_____

_____

_____

_____

_____

_____

_____

_____

_____

_____

_____

_____

_____

_____

_____

_____

_____

_____

_____

_____

_____

Day 27
CHOOSING LIFE

Declaration: "I CHOOSE LIFE!"

Scriptures of Worth, Confidence and Character:
"I call heaven and earth as witnesses today against you, that
I have set before you life and death, blessing and cursing;
therefore choose life, that both you and your descendants may
live; that you may love the Lord your God, that you may obey
His voice, and that you may cling to Him, for He is your life and
the length of your days;" *Deuteronomy 30: 19,20a NKJV.*

"Trust in the Lord with all your heart, and do not lean on your
own understanding. In all your ways acknowledge him, and
he will make straight your paths." *Proverbs 3:5,6 ESV*

Words of Worth, Confidence and Character:
Choices. We all make choices every day, all day. Some
choices are as simple as getting out of bed, brushing
your teeth, and eating your breakfast. Other choices
are more involved, like the decision to share, do your
chores and work hard in school. Choices can become
challenging when we think about the opportunity to tell
the truth versus tell a lie. Choices can get complicated,
when we choose to do something that we haven't asked
permission to do. This scripture in Deuteronomy speaks
about choices and how important they are to our lives.
To "choose life", is to choose God's way or God's plan
and to do what you know is right to do. It also means
using wisdom, common sense, and your best judgment
in any given situation. To "choose death", is to choose
anything outside of God's plan. It also means acting too
quickly or without carefully thinking through your actions
and how they will affect those around you. There is an
important thing to understand about choices- all choices

have consequences. Consequences are those little things that come along with any decision that we make. Consequences are the good results or bad results that happen because of the choices we make every day. It is important to know that your choices will not just affect you, but they will also directly or indirectly impact others.

Let me give you a simple example. One day while riding bikes with my family, I decided to do a bike trick that my dad would always do on his bike. He made it look so easy. I never practiced this trick, but I felt pretty confident that I could still do it. Dad made it look so cool. Well, I tried the bike trick for myself. It did not turn out well. Unfortunately, I lost control of the bike and I hit the ground pretty hard. I skinned my knees, (which really hurt), and I cried really hard. Looking back, I made the choice to do the bike trick, but it wasn't the smartest choice. I wasn't ready. I wasn't prepared. I had not practiced, and dad had never taught me how to safely perform this trick. What were my consequences? Two bloody, skinned knees and a lot of pain. Plus, our bike riding fun was over because I was hurt. My sister and brother were also upset with me for ruining our fun. I learned a valuable lesson that day. Bike riding was really fun and enjoyable, but if I wasn't careful, I could also get hurt on my bike.

There are many life lessons that come from the choices you make every day. Hopefully, as you lean into God's guidance throughout this journey, He can keep you from getting too many bloody, scraped up knees along the way. God wants you to be more aware of the choices that you make, and He wants you to use wisdom, common sense, advice from your parents and the scriptures to help you. God, as your Heavenly

Father, promises to direct you and lead you in the right direction. The scripture says, "do not lean on your own understanding, but in all your ways (choices) acknowledge Him and He will make straight your path". The choices you make right now, as a young person will directly impact your teen years and the choices you make during your teen years will directly impact your college years. Do you see a pattern? As you guessed, the choices you make during your college years will directly impact your adult life. Choices are very important. Choices are like the "Legos" of life. All your life choices stack up and connect in different ways. Our goal is for each of our choices to stack up and connect, building our lives into something special that honors God.

Think about this. Choosing to steal something versus choosing to pay for the item, might be a choice you are presented with. How will you choose? Choosing to quit your sport versus choosing to work hard and complete what you've started, might also be a choice you have to make. Choosing unhealthy behaviors versus taking care of your body, (which is God's temple), will definitely be a choice that you are presented with as a young person. You must learn how to choose life, even when others around you choose differently, which takes courage. What your friends choose to do should never replace what God and your parents have instructed you to do. You will make choices now and for the rest of your life. No situation is ever too big or too small for God. You can ask Him to help you choose the appropriate apps, books, magazines, music, movies, and games to download on your devices.

You can ask God to help you with anything. It is important to know that God doesn't expect perfection from you. We all make mistakes and sometimes poor choices. When this happens, He is waiting with open arms to still hear from you. Check this out. "But if we confess our sins, He is faithful and just to forgive us our sins and cleanse us from everything we've done wrong" (*1John 1:9 CEB*). If you make a poor choice, ask God for forgiveness, which He freely gives and be sure to learn from your mistakes. God loves you and making a mistake or a poor choice doesn't ever change that. He always wants to help you choose life in every decision that comes your way.

Prayer: I love you, Lord. Thank you for helping me to understand the importance of my choices. I choose life. I choose blessings. I choose to cling to You and listen to You, because You are my life, and You have good plans for my future. I trust You and I thank You for directing my steps, today and everyday into my future, in Jesus' name. Amen.

Parental/Adult Engagement:
What choices are You making right now, that will impact your future?

Personal Notes/Personal Thoughts:

_____

_____

_____

_____

_____

_____

_____

_____

Day 28
GUARDING MY HEART

Declaration: "I CHOOSE TO GUARD MY HEART!"

Scriptures of Worth, Confidence and Character:
"My son, pay attention to what I say; turn your ear to my words. Do not let them out of your sight, keep them within your heart; for they are life to those who find them and health to one's whole body. Above all else, guard your heart, for everything you do flows from it." *Proverbs 4: 20-23 NIV*

"My son, pay attention to my words. Bend your ear to my speech. Don't let them slip from your sight. Guard them in your mind. They are life to those who find them, and healing for their entire body. More than anything you guard, protect your mind, for life flows from it." *Proverbs 4:20-23 CEB*

"My son, give attention to my words; incline your ear to my sayings. Do not let them depart from your eyes; Keep them in the midst of your heart; For they are life to those who find them, and health to all their flesh. Keep your heart with all diligence, for out of it spring the issues of life." *Prov. 4:20-23 NKJV*

Words of Worth, Confidence and Character:
Guarding your heart is best summarized as the consistent work of being watchful about the things that your eyes and ears are allowed to see and hear. This is important because of the way that God has designed you. Your eyes and ears are the pathways into the heart. Your thoughts, emotions, words, actions, and habits are all formed from the very things you listen to and the very things you see through-out your life. The things that you hear and see, are the things that you "give attention to", which is why this scripture reminds us to "give attention to" God's words. Guarding your heart is a daily responsibility. It happens 24 hours a day, 7 days

a week and 365 days a year. Basically, you learn to do this all the time. While at home, at school, at a friend's house and even on vacation, guarding your heart should become natural to you. All 3 of the scriptures listed are saying the same thing, just in different ways. Your heart represents your life and because God cares deeply about your life, He wants you to protect your heart from negative images, words, places, or things. He wants you to fill your heart with good things, positive images, encouraging words, inspiring stories, and uplifting music. He wants you to experience places, activities and environments that stretch you to become all that He has created you to be.

At the end of my teen years, I wanted a deeper relationship with God. There was a hunger in me that only God could fill. I began to change the music I was listening to and started to listen to more music that encouraged and lifted my soul. This small change led to other positive changes in my life. Certain movies and shows, I chose not to see because I was in the process of growing up and learning to hear God's voice for myself. I wanted to become closer to God, and I needed to make some personal changes that would allow me to make better life choices. I began to understand the difference between the things that were negative for me versus the things that were beneficial for my eyes and ears. My choices, during that time in my life, were critical to the growth and the development of my relationship with God.

Have you ever noticed that 'feeling' you get when something is too romantic, too violent, or too scary for you? You may sense that uncomfortable feeling on the inside of you; that is God's way of helping you to recognize your boundaries. In those moments you should develop a strategy to help you guard your eyes and ears. In these situations, I have instructed my kids to leave the room, change the channel, or tell an adult. Your parents will be able to support you in this and give some suggestions as well. God loves you and wants you to begin to understand the importance of guarding your heart, which in turn will guard your life. I can't say this enough: fill your heart with good things, positive images, encouraging words, inspiring stories, and uplifting music. Pray about experiencing places, activities and environments that stretch you to become all that He has created you to be. Right now, begin to surround your life with God's words, God's thoughts, God's plans, God's purposes, and you will walk into the amazing future that He has for your life, even as a young person.

Prayer: I love You, Lord. I thank You for teaching me to guard my heart and in doing so, I am guarding my life. I trust You to help me in this process so that out of my heart will flow the purpose and plan You have for my life, in Jesus' name. Amen.

Parental/Adult Engagement: Have you ever noticed that 'feeling' you get when something is too romantic, too violent, or too scary for you? How can you begin the process of guarding your heart?

Personal Notes/Personal Thoughts:

_____

_____

_____

_____

_____

_____

_____

Day 29
WORDS HAVE POWER

Declaration: "MY WORDS HAVE POWER!"

Scriptures of Worth, Confidence and Character:
"Death and life are in the power of the tongue, and those who love it will eat its fruit." *Proverbs 18:21 NKJV*

"What you say can preserve life or destroy it; so you must accept the consequences of your words." *Proverbs 18:21 GNB*

Words of Worth, Confidence and Character:
A very important thing for you to know and understand as a young person, is that your words have power. You can encourage yourself or discourage yourself, with your own words. You can build yourself up or tear yourself down, with your own words. Your words can encourage and bless others, or your words can discourage and deflate others. Your words can build people up or tear people down. I always tell my girls, "...if you have nothing nice to say, say nothing at all." Mean words can destroy someone's self-esteem and self-worth. You must always choose your words wisely. God will help you to make good decisions with the words that you speak to yourself and to others. Always remember that the words you speak to yourself and about yourself are very important. Always use positive, uplifting, and inspiring words to motivate you. If you noticed, this book has specifically used the principle of the power of words, throughout each daily reading.

At the beginning of each reading, you make a positive declaration about yourself, for each day. Additionally, each word shared throughout this book has been carefully selected to bring you encouragement about your personal worth, character, and confidence in order to build your self-esteem. I want the words of this book to impact your thinking, your speaking and your behavior for years to come.

These words of worth, character and confidence will change your life forever, if you truly begin to allow them to sink into your heart and meditate on the scriptures and messages shared with you throughout this book. I hope that your parents, pastors, and other loved ones share words of strength, life, hope, love, grace, encouragement, inspiration, and courage with you now and for the rest of your life. It will require great focus from you to block out and reject words of failure, fear, discouragement, or discrimination. There will even be times when you will need to block out and reject thoughts and words of self-doubt, self-criticism, and comparison. God has intended for His words of love, confidence, wisdom, and faith to shape your life. Remember to always have the confidence to rise above these words and speak words of life over your future, your family, your friends, your academics, your health, and your circumstances. Words of life, like the scriptures and messages found in this book, will bring you into the good plans that God has for you.

Prayer: I love You, Lord. Thank You for helping me understand the power of the words that I speak. Your Word has power. Teach me how to speak Your Word over my life and to also use encouraging words to build myself up and to build up others, as well. In Jesus' name I pray. Amen.

Parental/Adult Engagement:
What words of confidence would you like to begin
speaking about yourself?

Personal Notes/Personal Thoughts:

_____

_____

_____

_____

_____

_____

_____

_____

_____

_____

_____

_____

_____

_____

_____

_____

_____

_____

_____

_____

_____

_____

_____

_____

_____

Day 30
RELATIONSHIP WITH GOD

Declaration: "I TREASURE MY RELATIONSHIP WITH GOD!"

Scriptures of Worth, Confidence and Character:
"For God so loved the world, that He gave His only begotten Son, that whoever believes in Him should not perish but have everlasting life." *John 3:16 NKJV*

"And it shall come to pass that whoever calls on the name of the Lord shall be saved." *Acts 2:21 NKJV*

"...if you confess with your mouth the Lord Jesus and believe in your heart that God has raised Him from the dead, you will be saved. For with the heart one believes unto righteousness, and with the mouth confession is made unto salvation." *Romans 10:9,10 NKJV*

Words of Worth, Confidence and Character:
God loves you very much, my friend. Honestly, He really loves you way more than you will ever realize. He loves you so much that He deeply desires to have a personal, intimate relationship with you, right now. The adults are cool, don't get me wrong. But He is not just interested in adults, like your mom, teacher or pastor. He is very interested in you, knowing Him. God doesn't want to be this mysterious, distant, unknown thing in your life. *James 4:8 NIV* says, "Come near to God and He will come near to you." He wants to be close with you and He doesn't ever want you to feel lonely or rejected. God sent His Son, Jesus to die for our sins and Jesus became our personal sacrifice. Now let me make that a personal statement for you. God sent His Son, Jesus to die for your sins and Jesus became your personal

sacrifice. He died for us because He wanted to wash us clean, from our sin, guilt, and shame.

When you recognize and understand this amazing truth, you can ask Jesus to come into your heart and become the Lord of your life. From there, you can begin a beautiful journey of a relationship with God, knowing He is walking with you every day and that your future and eternity is secure with Him. Dear friend, God is your greatest treasure, and you will never find anything more precious than Him.

Prayer For Salvation: I love You, Lord. I desire a relationship with You. Thank You for sending Jesus, to be my Lord, my Savior, and my sacrifice. I repent of my sins. Lord Jesus, come into my heart and be the Lord of my life. I confess that You died for my sins, and I believe that God raised You, Jesus from the dead and I am saved. I receive You, now. I surrender my life to You. Let Your will be done in my life, now and for the rest of my days, in Jesus' name. Amen.

Parental/Adult Engagement:
What are some ways that you can build your relationship with God?

Personal Notes/Personal Thoughts:

_____
_____
_____
_____
_____
_____
_____
_____
_____

THE SELF-CONFIDENCE DECLARATION

I, _____

DECLARE OVER MY LIFE THIS DAY THAT...

I AM AWESOME
I AM BRILLIANT
I AM CREATIVE
I AM DELIGHTFUL
I AM EXCELLENT
I AM FEARLESS
I AM GIFTED
I AM HELPFUL
I AM INTELLIGENT
I AM JOYFUL
I AM KIND
I AM LOVED
I AM MARVELOUS
I AM NICE
I AM OUTSTANDING
I AM PRECIOUS
I AM QUITE CLEVER
I AM RARE
I AM SPECIAL
I AM TALENTED
I AM UNIQUE
I AM VERY POLITE
I AM WONDERFUL
I AM EXQUISITE
I AM EXTRAORDINARY
I AM AMAZING
I CHOOSE LIFE
I CHOOSE TO GUARD MY HEART
MY WORDS HAVE POWER
I TREASURE MY RELATIONSHIP WITH GOD

I DECLARE THESE THINGS OVER MY LIFE, AND I WALK IN
SELF-CONFIDENCE BY HIS GRACE, IN JESUS' NAME. AMEN.

YOUR SIGNATURE: _____

DATE OF COMPLETION: _____

NOTES